"Healthcare Angels: Tales of Random Acts of Medicine"

Esme Laila

Table of Content:

Chapter 1: The Healing Touch: An Introduction to Random Acts of Medicine

Introduction:

In the vast and complex world of healthcare, where the focus is frequently on opinion, treatment, and procedures, there exists a special realm that goes beyond medical moxie. It's a realm where the mending touch of kindness, compassion, and empathy takes center stage. These are the stories of arbitrary acts of drug, the important moments when healthcare professionals and individualities selflessly reach out to make a difference in the lives of others. In this composition, we claw into the significance, impact, and exemplifications of these extraordinary acts, exploring how they shape the geography of healthcare.

Understanding Random Acts of Medicine

5

Random acts of drug can be defined as unanticipated gestures, both big and small, performed by healthcare professionals, levies, or indeed nonnatives, with the intention of perfecting the well- being of individualities in need. These acts transcend the boundaries of medical procedures and treatments, fastening rather on the mortal connection, emotional support, and genuine care that can profoundly impact cases and their families.

The Significance of Random Acts of Medicine

Random acts of drug hold immense significance within the healthcare field. While the core ideal of healthcare is to give medical treatment and palliate physical affections, these acts address the emotional, cerebral, and social aspects of mending. They remind us that compassionate care can play a vital part in a case's overall well- being and recovery process.

also, arbitrary acts of drug foster a sense of trust, comfort, and consolation between healthcare providers and cases. They humanize the healthcare experience, breaking down the walls that can frequently live in clinical settings. These acts not only bring solace and stopgap to those in need but also inspire others to emulate and immortalize kindness within the healthcare community.

exemplifications of Random Acts of Medicine

The Comforting Voice A nanny sits by the bedside of a alarmed case, holding their hand and speaking words of stimulant, furnishing a sense of comfort during a grueling time.

The Gift of Time A busy croaker takes a many redundant twinkles to engage in a genuine discussion with a case, laboriously harkening to their enterprises and offering emotional support, going beyond the constraints of a typical medical appointment.

The unanticipated Visit A croaker , after a long day at the sanitarium, makes an improvisational visit to check on a case at their home, icing durability of care and showing genuine concern beyond the sanitarium walls.

The Volunteer's Impact Levies selflessly offer their time and fellowship to cases, engaging in exchanges, playing games, or simply being there to give a harkening observance and a warm smile.

The Community's Response A group of healthcare professionals organizes a free health clinic in underserved areas, furnishing medical services, wireworks, and education to individualities who else would not have access tohealthcare.The Ripple Effect of Random Acts of Medicine Random acts of drug have a ripple effect that extends far beyond the immediate donors. When a healthcare professional goes over and beyond their call of duty to show compassion and kindness, it creates a positive impact that reverberates throughout the healthcare system. Cases who witness these acts of care frequently partake their stories, spreading alleviation and stopgap to others. also, witnessing or hearing about these acts motivates fellow healthcare professionals to reflect on their own practice, encouraging them to incorporate empathy and compassion into their diurnal relations with cases. The accretive effect of these acts contributes to a more compassionate and patient- centered healthcare terrain.

particular Connections that Restore quality
In a world where healthcare can occasionally feel impersonal and transactional, arbitrary acts of drug restore a sense of quality and humanity to cases. For individualities scuffling with illness, injury, or habitual conditions, the mending touch of a compassionate healthcare provider can give bottomless comfort. Whether it's a croaker taking the time to explain a complex opinion in simple terms, a nanny offering a harkening observance to a case's fears and enterprises, or a levy furnishing fellowship to palliate passions of insulation, these acts admit the person behind the illness and foster a sense of understanding and empathy.

Empowering Cases through Collaboration
Random acts of drug also empower cases to take an active part in their own

healthcare trip. When healthcare professionals engage in open and cooperative exchanges with cases, they produce an terrain that encourages participated decision- timber and fosters a sense of power over one's health. By involving cases in conversations about their treatment options, addressing their preferences and enterprises, and icing they've access to the information they need, arbitrary acts of drug empower cases to come lawyers for their well-being. This collaboration not only enhances the quality of care but also cultivates trust between cases and healthcare providers.

Going Beyond Borders and Boundaries Random acts of drug know no boundaries or borders. They transcend artistic, social, and profitable walls, feting that every existent deserves compassionate care, anyhow of their background or circumstances. These acts can be set up in civic hospitals, pastoral conventions, war-torn regions, and areas affected by natural disasters. Whether it's a levy medical platoon traveling to a developing country to give essential healthcare services or a original community organizing free conventions for underserved populations, arbitrary acts of drug illustrate the universal nature of compassion and the participated responsibility to watch for one another.

Inspiring Positive Change in Healthcare
The impact of arbitrary acts of drug extends beyond the immediate moment of care. They serve as catalysts for positive change within the healthcare system. These acts prompt reflection and dialogue among healthcare professionals, directors, and policymakers, pressing the significance of case- centered care and the need to prioritize empathy and compassion in healthcare settings. Through mindfulness juggernauts, training programs, and policy enterprise, healthcare associations and institutions can embrace and promote arbitrary acts of drug as an integral part of their morality, fostering a culture of kindness and empathy that permeates every aspect of the healthcare experience.

Chapter 2: Guardian Angels in Scrubs: Extraordinary Acts of Kindness

Introduction:

Within the healthcare profession, there are individualities who slip the noble part of guardian angels in diminutives, going over and beyond their call of duty to perform extraordinary acts of kindness. These acts of selflessness and compassion illustrate the true substance of healthcare, showcasing the remarkable impact that a single person can have on the lives of others. In this composition, we explore the stories and significance of these guardian angels, slipping light on their extraordinary acts and the profound goods they've on cases, families, and the healthcare community at large.

The substance of Guardian Angels in Scrubs

Guardian angels in diminutives are healthcare professionals who embody the spirit of compassion, empathy, and unwavering fidelity to their cases. They fete that mending extends beyond medical treatments and interventions, and they embrace the responsibility of furnishing holistic care that addresses the emotional, cerebral, and spiritual requirements of those they serve. These individualities retain a unique capability to connect with cases on a deep position, furnishing comfort, solace, and support during moments of vulnerability.

Extraordinary Acts of Kindness

Comfort in Times of Grief A guardian angel in scrubs sits with a grieving family member, offering a shoulder to cry on and furnishing a compassionate presence during the most delicate moments of loss.

Granting a Final Wish When faced with terminally ill cases, these guardian angels work lifelessly to fulfill their final wishes, whether it's arranging a bedside reunion with a loved one, easing a special experience, or creating a peaceful terrain for the end- of- life trip.

championing for Vulnerable Cases Guardian angels in diminutives go over and beyond to advocate for the rights and well- being of vulnerable populations, similar as championing for better healthcare access for underserved communities, championing for cases with language walls, or icing equal treatment and care for all cases.

easing Fears and Anxiety Feting the fear and anxiety that frequently accompany medical procedures, guardian angels in diminutives take the time to explain procedures in a compassionate and accessible manner, furnishing consolation and easing cases' enterprises.

Going the Extra Mile These healthcare professionals willingly go the redundant afar to meet the unique requirements of their cases, whether it's staying after hours to give fresh support, arranging technical services, or simply extending a harkening observance when cases need someone to talk to.

Acts of Compassion in Crisis Guardian angels in diminutives shine brightest during times of extremity, similar as natural disasters or mass casualties, where they parade extraordinary acts of kindness, working lifelessly to give care, comfort, and support to those affected.

The Profound Impact of Guardian Angels in Scrubs

The impact of these guardian angels extends far beyond the immediate acts of kindness. Their unvarying fidelity and exceptional care have profound goods on cases, their families, and the healthcare community as a whole.

Restoring Faith and Trust When cases encounter guardian angels in diminutives, they witness a restoration of faith and trust in the healthcare system. These acts of kindness support the belief that they aren't simply cases with medical conditions, but individualities earning of respect, quality, and substantiated care.

Emotional Healing and Well- being Extraordinary acts of kindness from guardian angels in diminutives contribute to the emotional mending and overall well- being of cases. By addressing the emotional and cerebral requirements, these acts foster a sense of comfort, security, and hope during grueling times.

Alleviation and commission Witnessing the selfless acts of these guardian angels inspires and empowers both cases and fellow healthcare professionals. Cases are motivated to overcome adversity, find strength in their trip, and indeed pay forward the kindness they've entered. Healthcare professionals are inspired to embrace the values of compassion and empathy, leading to a further compassionate healthcare culture.

Strengthening the Case- Provider Relationship The acts of kindness from guardian angels in diminutives foster stronger bonds between cases and healthcare providers. Cases feel a deeper connection and trust with their caregivers, which leads to bettered communication, enhanced patient satisfaction, and eventually, better healthcare issues.

Cultivating a Culture of Compassion The presence of guardian angels in diminutives within healthcare institutions cultivates a culture of compassion, where acts of kindness aren't only conceded but also encouraged and celebrated. This culture permeates throughout the association, appreciatively impacting the entire healthcare platoon and leading to an terrain where compassion becomes an essential part of the care handed.

Chapter 3: When Compassion Takes the Lead: Nurses' Stories of Care

Introduction:

Nursing is a profession embedded in compassion and empathy, where devoted healthcare professionals strive to give holistic care to cases. When compassion takes the lead, nursers come important lawyers, healers, and pillars of support. In this composition, we explore the profound impact of compassionate nursing through inspiring stories of nursers who go over and beyond their call of duty. These stories showcase the transformative power of empathy and compassion in nursing practice, as well as the deep connection nursers form with their cases.

The substance of Compassionate Nursing

Compassionate nursing is at the heart of case- centered care. It encompasses not only the specialized chops and medical knowledge that nursers retain but also the capability to truly connect with cases on an emotional position. It involves active listening, genuine empathy, and the amenability to understand the unique requirements, fears, and bournes of each existent in their care. When compassion takes the lead, nursers come healers who give comfort, support, and understanding to cases and their families.

Stories of Compassionate Nursing

The Comforting Presence In the bustling terrain of a sanitarium, a compassionate nanny takes the time to sit with a case, holding their hand and furnishing emotional support. Through their presence, the nanny helps palliate anxiety and offers a sense of consolation, creating a safe space for the case to express their enterprises.

championing for Cases A compassionate nanny becomes a fierce advocate for a case who's floundering to communicate their requirements. The nanny goes over and beyond to insure the case's voice is heard, uniting with the healthcare platoon and championing for the necessary coffers to meet the case's unique conditions.

Empathy in Times of Grief In the face of loss, a compassionate nanny extends sincere empathy to the family members left before. They give solace, offering a harkening observance, and allowing the family members to partake recollections, fears, and feelings. Through their presence and understanding, the nanny helps the family navigate the delicate trip of grief.

Going Beyond the Medical A compassionate nanny recognizes that mending extends beyond physical affections. They take the time to understand the case's emotional and spiritual requirements, offering words of stimulant, prayer, or simply being a compassionate presence during times of torture.

Cultivating Trust A nanny builds a trusting relationship with a case by laboriously harkening, treating them with respect and quality, and involving them in their care opinions. Through their compassionate approach, the nanny fosters an terrain of trust and open communication, allowing the case to laboriously share in their mending process.

The Impact of Compassionate Nursing

The impact of compassionate nursing extends far beyond individual patient relations. It influences patient issues, healthcare surroundings, and the overall well- being of nursers themselves.

Advanced Case issues Compassionate nursing has been linked to bettered patient issues. When cases feel authentically watched for, heeded to, and understood, they're more likely to misbehave with treatment plans, laboriously engage in their own care, and experience more physical and emotional well- being.

Enhancing Case Satisfaction Compassionate nursing significantly contributes to patient satisfaction. Cases who admit compassionate care feel valued, admired, and supported during their healthcare trip. This positive experience enhances their overall satisfaction with the healthcare system and promotes a sense of trust in their nursing providers.

Strengthening nanny- Case connections Compassionate nursing builds strong nanny - case connections grounded on trust, empathy, and open communication. These connections foster a sense of cooperation and collaboration, empowering cases to laboriously share in their care opinions. nursers who prioritize compassion produce an terrain that allows for substantiated care and tailors interventions to meet the specific requirements of each case.

easing Case Anxiety and Fear Compassionate nursing plays a pivotal part in easing patient anxiety and fear. By furnishing emotional support, harkening attentively, and offering explanations in a compassionate manner, nursers help cases feel more at ease and reduce the stress associated with healthcare hassles.

Emotional Well- being of nursers Engaging in compassionate care not only benefits cases but also enhances the emotional well- being of nursers themselves. nursers who prioritize compassion in their practice frequently report increased job satisfaction, a sense of purpose, and a deep fulfillment deduced from making a positive impact on the lives of others.

Shaping a Culture of Compassion Compassionate nursing has the implicit to shape the culture within healthcare associations. When empathy and compassion are valued and promoted, nursers and other healthcare professionals are inspired to embrace a analogous approach in their practice. This fosters a culture of compassion that permeates throughout the healthcare terrain, serving both cases and the entire healthcare platoon.

Chapter 4: Doctors on a Mission: Going Above and Beyond for Patients

Introduction:

Croakers are frequently regarded as the epitome of medical moxie and clinical knowledge. still, there are exceptional croakers
who go beyond their professional liabilities and embrace a charge to give extraordinary care to their cases. These croakers
are driven by a deep commitment to their cases' well- being and are willing to go over and beyond to insure their cases admit the loftiest position of care. In this composition, we claw into the stories of croakers
on a charge, exploring the ways in which they surpass prospects, the impact they've on cases' lives, and the transformative effect they bring to the field of drug.

The substance of Croakers on a Mission

Croakers on a charge are driven by a profound fidelity to their cases' weal. They fete that their part extends beyond medical moxie, encompassing compassion, empathy, and a commitment to perfecting the lives of those under their care. These croakers see themselves as lawyers, healers, and mates in their cases' peregrinations, going beyond the call of duty to give exceptional care and support.

Going Beyond Medical Expertise

structure Trusting connections Croakers on a charge prioritize structure trusting connections with their cases. They take the time to hear attentively, communicate easily, and address cases' enterprises, fostering an terrain where cases feel comfortable participating their medical history, fears, and expedients.

Holistic Care Feting that mending involves further than just physical affections, croakers on a charge give holistic care. They consider cases' emotional, cerebral, and social well- being, taking into account the impact of these factors on their overall health and recovery.

Case Advocacy These croakers act as strong lawyers for their cases, icing they admit the stylish possible care and treatment. They go to great lengths to navigate complex healthcare systems, unite with other specialists, and communicate effectively with cases and their families, all in the pursuit of optimal issues.

personalized Treatment Plans Croakers on a charge understand that every case is unique, and they knitter treatment plans to suit individual requirements. They consider cases' preferences, values, and artistic backgrounds, icing that their medical opinions are aligned with the case's overall well- being and particular circumstances.

Going the Extra Mile Croakers on a charge willingly go over and beyond to give exceptional care. Whether it's working long hours, conducting expansive exploration, or seeking innovative treatment options, they do whatever it takes to offer their cases the stylish chance of recovery and bettered quality of life.

Inspiring Stories of Croakers on a Mission

Breaking Boundaries In remote and underserved areas, croakers on a charge leave the comfort of established medical centers and trip to remote communities to give essential healthcare services. They frequently face grueling conditions and limited coffers but remain undeterred in their charge to bring healthcare to those who need it most.

Global Medical Outreach Some croakers on a charge devote their chops to global medical outreach, traveling to developing countries to give medical care and education. They unite with original healthcare professionals, train original staff, and address critical healthcare needs in underserved communities around the world.

Innovating for Better Care Croakers on a charge strive to ameliorate medical care by pursuing innovative results. They engage in exploration, develop new ways, and advocate for advancements in their separate fields. Their commitment to advancing medical knowledge translates into better treatment options and bettered issues for their cases.

Case- Centered exploration Croakers on a charge laboriously engage in case-centered exploration, fastening on chancing answers to unmet medical requirements and perfecting the quality of care. By involving cases in exploration and clinical trials, they insure that medical advancements are guided by the gests and perspectives of those directly affected by the conditions being studied.

The Impact of Croakers on a Mission

Advanced Case issues Croakers on a charge have a significant impact on patient issues. Their exceptional care and fidelity contribute to better treatment adherence, bettered recovery rates, and enhanced overall health issues for their cases.

Empowered Cases By going over and further for their cases, croakers on a charge empower cases to take an active part in their own healthcare. Through effective communication, participated decision- timber, and patient education, they equip cases with the knowledge and confidence to make informed choices about their treatment and care.

Inspired Healthcare Professionals The conduct of croakers
on a charge inspire other healthcare professionals, both within their own specialties and across the medical field. Their commitment to exceptional care sets a standard of excellence, encouraging others to strive for analogous situations of fidelity and compassion in their own practice.

Influence on Healthcare Systems Croakers on a charge challenge and influence healthcare systems, championing for case- centered care, bettered access to healthcare, and indifferent distribution of coffers. Their sweats punctuate the significance of holistic care and can lead to positive changes in healthcare programs and practices.

Transformation of the Croaker- Case
Relationship Through their exceptional
care, croakers
on a charge transfigure the croaker
- case relationship. They foster trust,
empathy, and open communication,
performing in a cooperation that
empowers cases to laboriously share in
their own care and eventually leads to
bettered patient satisfaction.

Chapter 5: Unsung Heroes: Support Staff and their Impactful Acts

Introduction:

Within the healthcare system, there are innumerous individualities who work diligently behind the scenes, furnishing essential support to insure the smooth operation of medical installations. From custodians and executive labor force to conservation workers and transport staff, these obscure icons play a vital part in delivering quality case care. In this composition, we explore the stories of support staff and their poignant acts, slipping light on their inestimable benefactions and the profound impact they've on cases, healthcare professionals, and the overall healthcare experience.

The significance of Support Staff

Support staff form the backbone of the healthcare system, fulfilling critical places that frequently go uncelebrated. Their liabilities encompass a wide range of tasks, including maintaining cleanliness, organizing paperwork, coordinating logistics, furnishing transportation, and much further. Without their inexhaustible sweats, the flawless operation of healthcare installations would be significantly compromised. Support staff produce an terrain conducive to mending, icing that healthcare professionals can concentrate on their core liabilities of furnishing patient care.

poignant Acts of Support Staff

Creating a Drinking Environment Support staff are frequently the first point of contact for cases and callers. They hail individualities with warmth, kindness, and a friendly smile, setting a positive tone and creating a welcoming atmosphere that promotes a sense of comfort and ease.

Maintaining Cleanliness and Safety Custodial and housekeeping staff work diligently to maintain cleanliness and sanitation norms within healthcare installations. Their sweats play a pivotal part in precluding infections and icing a safe terrain for cases, callers, and healthcare professionals.

Streamlining executive Processes executive staff handle colorful executive tasks, similar as scheduling movables , managing medical records, and coordinating paperwork. Their effectiveness and attention to detail contribute to the smooth functioning of healthcare operations, allowing healthcare professionals to concentrate on patient care.

Easing Effective Logistics Transport staff, including ambulance motorists and medical couriers, insure the safe and timely transportation of cases and medical inventories. Their trustability and moxie enable the flawless movement of individualities and critical coffers, supporting the overall functioning of the healthcare system.

furnishing Emotional Support Support staff, similar as receptionists and levies, offer a comforting presence and a harkening observance to cases and their families. They understand the anxieties and enterprises that individualities may face and give emotional support, helping to palliate stress and fostering a compassionate terrain.

Nurturing a Healing Environment conservation workers insure that healthcare installations are well-maintained, creating a clean, functional, and aesthetically pleasing terrain. By tending to outfit, fixing structural issues, and creating comfortable spaces, they contribute to a mending terrain that promotes patient well- being.

The Profound Impact of Support Staff

Case Experience and Satisfaction The poignant acts of support staff significantly impact the patient experience and overall satisfaction with healthcare services. From the moment cases enter the installation to their relations throughout their trip, support staff shape the terrain and contribute to positive gests that inseminate trust, comfort, and a sense of care.

Enhanced effectiveness and Productivity The sweats of support staff streamline executive processes, manage logistics, and maintain cleanliness. By doing so, they enable healthcare professionals to concentrate on delivering quality care, performing in bettered effectiveness and productivity within healthcare settings.

Collaboration and cooperation Support staff foster collaboration and cooperation within healthcare brigades. Their relations with healthcare professionals produce a sense of fellowship, collective respect, and appreciation for the integral part each person plays in furnishing comprehensive care.

Emotional Well- being of Cases and Staff The poignant acts of support staff contribute to the emotional well- being of both cases and healthcare professionals. Cases feel assured, supported, and valued, which can palliate anxiety and promote a positive mending experience. contemporaneously, healthcare professionals profit from the cooperative and compassionate terrain created by support staff, leading to increased job satisfaction and overall well- being.

Positive Organizational Culture The collaborative sweats of support staff shape the culture and morality of healthcare associations. Their fidelity, hard work, and commitment to excellence set the standard for a culture that values cooperation, empathy, and case- centered care. This positive organizational culture permeates throughout the healthcare system, serving all those involved.

Recognition and Appreciation
Acknowledging and appreciating the poignant acts of support staff creates a culture of gratefulness within healthcare settings. Feting their benefactions uplifts morale, promotes a sense of belonging, and strengthens the overall sense of community among healthcare professionals.

Chapter 6: The Gift of Time: Volunteers and Their Selfless Service

Introduction:

Levies play a vital part in colorful aspects of society, and the realm of healthcare is no exception. Their selfless service and fidelity make a significant impact on the lives of cases, their families, and healthcare professionals. In this composition, we explore the profound donation of levies in the healthcare sector and claw into the ways in which their gift of time and compassion enhances the well- being of individualities and the overall healthcare experience.

Understanding the part of Levies in Healthcare

Levies in healthcare are individualities who freehandedly contribute their time, chops, and moxie to support cases, families, and healthcare institutions. They serve as a vital link between healthcare professionals and the community, offering backing, fellowship, and emotional support to those in need. While their places and liabilities may vary, the common thread that unites them is their unvarying fidelity to making a positive difference in the lives of others.

The Impactful Acts of Healthcare Levies

Emotional Support for Cases Levies give emotional support by offering fellowship, advancing a harkening observance, and engaging in meaningful exchanges with cases. They bring comfort, empathy, and a sense of normality during grueling times, easing passions of loneliness, anxiety, and insulation.

backing to Healthcare Professionals Levies play a supporting part by aiding healthcare professionals in colorful tasks, similar as running errands, organizing inventories, or easing patient conditioning. By doing so, they free up precious time for healthcare providers to concentrate on furnishing direct case care.

Case Advocacy Levies serve as lawyers for cases, icing their requirements and enterprises are heard and addressed.

They give precious feedback to healthcare professionals, helping to ameliorate the quality of care and the patient experience.

fellowship for Elderly or insulated Cases Levies frequently spend time with senior or isolated cases who may have limited social relations. They engage in exchanges, play games, read books, or simply offer a comforting presence, cheering the cases' day and combating passions of loneliness.

Support for Families Levies extend their backing and support to the families of cases. They offer guidance, give information, and act as a source of comfort during times of stress and query.

Community Outreach and Education Levies contribute to community outreach enterprise, raising mindfulness about healthcare issues, promoting preventative care, and furnishing education on motifs similar as healthy living and complaint forestallment.

The Profound Impact of Volunteer Service

Enhanced Case Experience The selfless service of levies significantly enhances the patient experience within healthcare settings. Their compassionate presence, attentive listening, and acts of kindness produce a probative terrain that promotes emotional well- being and fosters a sense of belonging.

Improved Mental and Emotional Well- being Levies' fidelity to furnishing emotional support appreciatively impacts the internal and emotional well- being of cases. By offering fellowship and engaging in meaningful relations, they contribute to reduced stress, bettered mood, and increased adaptability among cases.

Reduced Healthcare difference Volunteer services can help bridge the gap in healthcare difference by reaching underserved communities and populations with limited access to care. Their sweats give essential support and coffers to those who may else go without necessary healthcare services.

Relief for Healthcare Professionals Levies palliate the workload of healthcare professionals, enabling them to concentrate on furnishing direct medical care. This backing not only improves effectiveness but also helps to help collapse among healthcare staff.

Sense of Fulfillment and Purpose
Volunteering in healthcare provides individualities with a sense of fulfillment, purpose, and particular growth. Levies frequently report increased satisfaction and a deep sense of gratefulness for the occasion to make a positive impact on the lives of others.

Strengthening Community Connections
The involvement of levies strengthens the bond between healthcare institutions and the girding community. Through their service, levies come ministers, fostering a sense of trust, collaboration, and goodwill between healthcare providers and the community they serve.

Inspiring Others The selfless acts of levies inspire others to contribute to their communities and make a difference. By witnessing the impact of levy service, individualities are encouraged to step forward and offer their time and chops, leading to a ripple effect of compassion and kindness.

Chapter 7: Acts of Empathy: Listening and Understanding Patients' Needs

Introduction:

Empathy is a abecedarian aspect of furnishing quality healthcare. It goes further simply diagnosing and treating medical conditions; it involves truly harkening to cases and understanding their requirements on a deeper position. This essay will explore the significance of acts of empathy in healthcare, with a particular focus on the skill of active listening and its impact on patient issues. By laboriously harkening and understanding cases' requirements, healthcare providers can produce a trusting and probative terrain that enhances patient satisfaction and improves overall healthcare gests .

Understanding Empathy in Healthcare

Empathy in healthcare refers to the capability of healthcare providers to understand and partake the passions and gests of their cases. It involves placing oneself in the case's shoes and viewing the world from their perspective. Acts of empathy in healthcare have been shown to increase patient satisfaction, ameliorate treatment adherence, and indeed enhance clinical issues. thus, it's pivotal for healthcare professionals to develop and upgrade their empathy chops, with a specific focus on effective listening.

The Power of Active harkening

Active listening is a crucial element of compassionate communication. It involves completely concentrating on, understanding, and responding to the case's verbal andnon-verbal cues. Active listening requires healthcare providers to be present in the moment, suspending judgment, and creating a safe space for cases to express their enterprises and requirements. By laboriously harkening, healthcare providers can gather essential information, make fellowship, and establish trust with their cases.

Creating a safe-deposit box and probative terrain
When healthcare providers laboriously hear to their cases, it creates an terrain where cases feel safe and supported. Cases may have anxieties, fears, or indeed embarrassment about their health enterprises. By harkening attentively, healthcare providers demonstrate their commitment to understanding the case's unique circumstances, fostering a sense of trust and compassion. This safe terrain encourages cases to partake their gests openly, leading to more accurate judgments and acclimatized treatment plans.

Gathering Comprehensive Case Information
Active listening allows healthcare providers to gain comprehensive patient information beyond the medical history. Cases frequently give precious perceptivity into their symptoms, gests , and enterprises that may not be apparent in a clinical examination. These details can help healthcare providers more understand the case's condition, make further informed opinions, and give

substantiated care. also, active listening helps uncover any social, artistic, or cerebral factors that may impact the case's well- being, enabling a holistic approach to healthcare.

Enhancing Case Satisfaction and Engagement
Cases who feel heard and understood are more likely to be satisfied with their healthcare gests . Active listening reassures cases that their enterprises are valid and that their healthcare provider authentically cares about their well- being. This, in turn, enhances patient engagement and collaboration. When cases laboriously share in their care, they're more likely to cleave to treatment plans, follow medical advice, and achieve better health issues.

Building Trust and Strengthening the Case- Provider Relationship
The case- provider relationship is erected on trust. Active listening plays a vital part in establishing and nurturing this trust. By laboriously harkening, healthcare providers demonstrate respect for the case's autonomy and validate their gests . This fosters a stronger bond between the

case and provider, leading to bettered communication, participated decision- timber, and eventually, better health issues.

relating unvoiced Needs
frequently, cases may have unvoiced requirements that go beyond their immediate medical enterprises. These requirements could include emotional support, consolation, or information about their condition. Through active listening, healthcare providers can identify these unvoiced requirements and address them meetly. By admitting and responding to these requirements, healthcare providers can offer a further comprehensive and patient- centered approach to watch.

Chapter 8: From the Streets to the ER: Random Acts of Medicine for the Homeless

Introduction:

Homelessness is a complex issue affecting millions of individualities worldwide. Living on the thoroughfares exposes homeless individualities to multitudinous health pitfalls and challenges, frequently leading to poor physical and internal well- being. In response to this extremity, arbitrary acts of drug have surfaced as a important means of furnishing healthcare to those who are homeless. This essay explores the significance and impact of arbitrary acts of drug for the homeless population, pressing the unique challenges they face and the colorful enterprise aimed at addressing their healthcare needs.

Understanding the Healthcare Challenges of the Homeless

Homelessness presents a myriad of healthcare challenges that significantly impact the well- being of individualities on the thoroughfares. The homeless population frequently lacks access to regular medical care, preventative services, and introductory musts like clean water, sanitation, and nutritional food. also, homeless individualities are more vulnerable to internal health diseases, substance abuse, contagious conditions, and habitual conditions due to limited coffers and exposure to harsh living conditions. Addressing these challenges requires targeted sweats that extend beyond traditional healthcare settings.

The part of Random Acts of Medicine

Random acts of drug for the homeless involve furnishing healthcare services, including medical consultations, preventative care, vaccinations, and hygiene support, through mobile conventions, outreach programs, and levy enterprise. These acts aim to ground the healthcare gap for the homeless population, icing they admit the necessary medical attention, support, and coffers to ameliorate their health issues. Random acts of drug have the eventuality to reach individualities who are doubtful to seek care through conventional means and can make a significant impact on their lives.

Mobile Conventions and Outreach Programs

Mobile conventions and outreach programs are crucial factors of arbitrary acts of drug for the homeless. These enterprise bring healthcare directly to the thoroughfares, harbors, and community centers visited by homeless individualities. Equipped with medical inventories, healthcare professionals, and support staff, these mobile conventions offer a range of services, including introductory health wireworks, crack care, vaccinations, and referrals to technical care when demanded. By taking healthcare services to where homeless individualities live, mobile conventions insure that indeed the most marginalized populations have access to medical attention and preventative care.

Street Medicine Programs

Street drug programs are specialized enterprise that give medical care to individualities living on the thoroughfares. These programs emplace healthcare professionals, similar as croakers
, nursers, and social workers, who laboriously engage with homeless individualities in their own surroundings. By erecting trust and establishing connections, road drug programs can address immediate health enterprises, offer advice on managing habitual conditions, give comforting for internal health and substance abuse issues, and connect individualities with necessary coffers, similar as harbors, food banks, and social services. Street drug programs empower healthcare providers to reach out to the homeless population with empathy, understanding, and compassion.

Collaborations with Community Organizations

Random acts of drug for the homeless frequently involve collaborations between healthcare providers and community associations that specialize in addressing homelessness. These hookups enable a comprehensive approach to watch, combining medical services with social support. For illustration, healthcare providers may team up with homeless harbors to offer on- point medical conventions or mate with haze kitchens to give nutrition education and hygiene accoutrements . By working together, these collaborations insure that healthcare services are integrated into the broader sweats of supporting and upping homeless individualities.

Volunteer Initiatives
Random acts of drug for the homeless heavily calculate on the fidelity and compassion of levies. Levies can come from colorful backgrounds, including healthcare professionals, medical scholars, and community members passionate about making a difference. These levies contribute their time, chops, and coffers to give healthcare services, distribute inventories, and offer emotional support to homeless individualities. Volunteer enterprise not only expand the reach of arbitrary acts of drug but also raise mindfulness about homelessness and foster a sense of

community engagement in addressing this issue.

Advocacy and Policy Change
Random acts of drug for the homeless also play a vital part in championing for policy changes that address the root causes of homelessness and ameliorate access to healthcare. By furnishing direct care to the homeless population, healthcare providers substantiation firsthand the impact of shy casing, poverty, and limited healthcare coffers. These gests and perceptivity can be abused to advocate for programs that prioritize affordable casing, comprehensive healthcare services, internal health support, and social safety nets. Through advocacy sweats, arbitrary acts of drug for the homeless contribute to systemic changes that profit not only individual homeless individualities but the entire community.

Chapter 9: Delivering Hope: Random Acts of Medicine in Remote Areas

Introduction:

Access to healthcare is a abecedarian mortal right, yet millions of people in remote areas around the world warrant acceptable medical services. Remote areas are frequently characterized by geographical walls, limited structure, and failure of healthcare professionals. In response to this challenge, arbitrary acts of drug have surfaced as a important means of delivering healthcare services to remote communities. This essay explores the significance and impact of arbitrary acts of drug in remote areas, pressing the unique challenges faced by these communities and the colorful enterprise aimed at bridging the healthcare gap.

Understanding the Healthcare Challenges in Remote Areas

Remote areas present distinct healthcare challenges that make access to medical services delicate for the original population. Geographical insulation, long distances, and grueling terrain make it laborious for individualities to reach healthcare installations. Limited structure, including shy roads, transportation, and communication systems, further complicate the problem. also, remote communities frequently face a deficit of healthcare professionals who are reticent to work in these areas due to the lack of coffers and insulation. These challenges bear innovative approaches to deliver healthcare services effectively.

The part of Random Acts of Medicine

Random acts of drug in remote areas involve furnishing healthcare services, preventative care, health education, and essential medical inventories through mobile conventions, community outreach, and levy enterprise. These acts aim to address the specific healthcare requirements of remote communities and insure that individualities in these areas have access to quality medical care. Random acts of drug are frequently carried out by devoted healthcare professionals, levies, and associations committed to making a difference in remote regions.

Mobile Conventions and Outreach Programs
Mobile conventions and outreach programs are vital factors of arbitrary acts of drug in remote areas. These enterprise bring medical professionals, inventories, and outfit directly to the communities, barring the walls of distance and transportation. Equipped with essential medical tools, mobile conventions give a range of services, including general check- ups, vaccinations, introductory treatments, and health education. These programs are designed to reach the most isolated communities, icing that indeed the most vulnerable individualities admit the care they need.

Telemedicine and Technology
Advancements in technology have converted the delivery of healthcare services in remote areas. Telemedicine allows healthcare professionals to ever connect with cases in remote

communities, furnishing consultations, diagnosing conditions, and offering guidance. Through videotape conferencing, remote monitoring bias, and digital health records, telemedicine enables healthcare providers to ground the distance gap and deliver healthcare services effectively. also, the use of mobile apps and telecommunication tools facilitates health education, mindfulness juggernauts, and access to medical information, empowering individualities in remote areas to take control of their health.

Collaborations with Original Communities Random acts of drug in remote areas frequently involve collaborations with original communities to insure sustainable and culturally applicable healthcare delivery. Working nearly with community leaders, associations gain a deeper understanding of the specific healthcare requirements, artistic beliefs, and practices of the original population. This knowledge helps knitter healthcare services to the unique conditions of the community and promotes community participation in healthcare enterprise. By involving original communities, arbitrary acts of drug foster power and sustainability, empowering individualities to take charge of their health and well-being.

Capacity structure and Training
To address the deficit of healthcare professionals in remote areas, arbitrary acts of drug focus on capacity structure and training enterprise. These programs aim to empower original healthcare providers, community health workers, and levies with the knowledge and chops necessary to deliver quality healthcare services. Training programs encompass a wide range of motifs, including introductory medical care, preventative measures, exigency response, and health creation. By equipping original individualities with the necessary chops, arbitrary acts of drug contribute to the long- term sustainability of healthcare services in remote areas.

Advocacy and Policy Change
Random acts of drug in remote areas not only give immediate healthcare relief but also endorse for policy changes and systemic advancements. These enterprise frequently exfoliate light on the

healthcare difference faced by remote communities and the need for indifferent access to medical services. By establishing the challenges, success stories, and impact of their interventions, associations engaged in arbitrary acts of drug can impact policymakers and advocate for the allocation of coffers, structure development, and healthcare programs that prioritize the requirements of remote areas.

Chapter 10: A Healing Hand for Children: Pediatric Tales of Compassion

Introduction:

Pediatric healthcare is a unique and vital branch of drug that focuses on the care and well- being of children. Children frequently bear technical medical attention due to their unique physiology, experimental requirements, and vulnerability. Compassion plays a central part in pediatric care, as healthcare providers work lifelessly to palliate the pain and suffering of youthful cases. This essay explores the significance and impact of compassion in pediatric healthcare, pressing the tales of compassion that unfold in the treatment of children.

Understanding the significance of Compassion in Pediatric Healthcare

Compassion is the foundation of pediatric healthcare, as it shapes the way healthcare providers interact with children and their families. Children are particularly vulnerable when facing illness or injury, and compassionate care not only improves their physical well-being but also helps reduce fear, anxiety, and emotional torture. Compassionate healthcare providers hear attentively, validate children's gests , and engage in age-applicable communication to make trust and establish a mending terrain. By embodying compassion, pediatric healthcare providers can make a profound difference in the lives of children and their families.

Tales of Compassion in Pediatric Healthcare

Comforting and Soothing In pediatric healthcare, healthcare providers frequently go over and beyond to console and soothe children during medical procedures. This may involve using distraction ways, similar as liar or playing music, to deflect children's attention down from discomfort. Compassionate healthcare providers take the time to explain procedures in a child-friendly manner, furnishing consolation and answering questions to palliate fear and anxiety.

Emotional Support Children facing medical challenges frequently witness a wide range of feelings, from fear and sadness to frustration and wrathfulness. Compassionate healthcare providers produce a safe and probative space for children to express their feelings. They offer empathy, active listening, and confirmation of children's passions, helping them navigate their emotional trip and furnishing comfort during delicate times.

Collaboration with Families Compassionate pediatric healthcare extends beyond the child to include the family as a whole. Healthcare providers fete the vital part of parents and caregivers in a child's mending process. They involve families in decision- timber, admire their artistic beliefs and values, and give emotional support and guidance. By uniting with families, healthcare providers produce a cooperation that enhances the child's overall well- being and treatment issues.

Going the Extra Mile Tales of compassion in pediatric healthcare frequently involve healthcare providers going the redundant afar to insure children's comfort and well-being. This may include substantiated gestures, similar as bringing a favorite toy, arranging visits from remedy creatures, or creating a child-friendly terrain within the healthcare setting. These acts of compassion bring joy, normality, and a sense of security to children during their medical trip.

Palliative and End- of- Life Care Compassion plays a pivotal part in supporting children and families facing serious ails or end- of- life care. Healthcare providers work collaboratively with families to give compassionate and staid care, icing that children and their loved bones are comfortable and supported. They address not only physical symptoms but also emotional and spiritual requirements, allowing families to find solace and meaning during delicate times.

The Impact of Compassion in Pediatric Healthcare

Compassion in pediatric healthcare has far- reaching goods on the well- being and issues of children and their families.

Trust and Communication Compassionate care builds trust between healthcare providers, children, and families. When children feel heard, understood, and watched for, they're more likely to engage in open communication with healthcare providers, share pivotal information, and laboriously share in their care. This leads to advanced treatment adherence, better health issues, and enhanced overall case satisfaction.

Emotional Well- being Compassionate care appreciatively impacts children's emotional well- being during their medical trip. By addressing their emotional requirements and fears, healthcare providers can reduce anxiety and torture, promoting a sense of calm and security. This emotional support not only enhances the child's managing capacities but also contributes to their overall cerebral adaptability.

Long- term Relationship Compassionate care fosters long- term connections between healthcare providers, children, and families. These connections go beyond the immediate medical hassle and produce a sense of durability and trust. When children and families have a positive and compassionate healthcare experience, they're more likely to seek ongoing care, follow up on treatments, and establish a medical home for their unborn healthcare requirements.

Family- Centered Care Compassion in pediatric healthcare recognizes the significance of family involvement and supports a family- centered approach. By laboriously involving families in decision-timber, furnishing emotional support, and valuing their input, healthcare providers empower families to come lawyers for their child's health and well- being. This collaboration enhances treatment issues and supports the holistic requirements of the child and their family.

Chapter 11: Moments of Comfort: Palliative Care and End-of-Life Random Acts

Introduction:

Palliative care and end- of- life support are essential factors of healthcare that concentrate on furnishing comfort, quality, and emotional support to individualities facing serious illness and the end of life. While these moments can be grueling , arbitrary acts of kindness and compassion have the power to make a significant impact on cases and their families during this sensitive time. This essay explores the significance and impact of arbitrary acts of palliative care and end- of- life support, pressing the moments of comfort that arise from these acts.

Understanding Palliative Care and End- of- Life Support

Palliative care aims to ameliorate the quality of life for cases facing serious ails by addressing their physical, emotional, and spiritual requirements. It focuses on pain and symptom operation, enhancing comfort, and furnishing support to cases and their families. End- of- life support encompasses care handed to individualities in their final stages of life, icing that they admit compassionate and staid care while addressing their unique requirements and preferences.

The part of Random Acts in Palliative Care and End- of- Life Support

Random acts in palliative care and end- of- life support involve acts of kindness, empathy, and compassion that give comfort, support, and moments of solace for cases and their families. These acts go beyond traditional medical interventions, fastening on the emotional and spiritual well- being of individualities during their trip. Random acts in this environment end to enhance the quality of life, produce positive recollections, and offer a sense of peace and comfort during grueling times.

Creating a Calming Environment
Random acts in palliative care and end- of- life support frequently involve

creating a soothing and comforting terrain for cases. This may include arranging substantiated decorations, playing soft music, furnishing comfortable coverlet, or creating a peaceful air through lighting and aromatherapy. These small gestures help produce a sense of serenity and tranquility, fostering a peaceful and comfortable terrain for cases and their loved bones

.

Presence and Companionship
The presence of compassionate individualities can make a significant difference in the lives of cases and their families during palliative care and end-of- life moments. Random acts may involve levies or healthcare professionals who give fellowship, a harkening observance, or simply being present with cases and their families. This fellowship offers emotional support, consolation, and a sense of comfort during delicate times.

Emotional Support for Cases and Families
Random acts of emotional support give comfort and solace to cases and their families during their trip. These acts may

involve holding hands, offering gentle traces, or furnishing a shoulder to lean on. Compassionate healthcare providers or levies engage in active listening, validating cases' passions and enterprises, and furnishing emotional support acclimatized to individual requirements. This empathy and understanding palliate anxiety, fear, and insulation, promoting moments of comfort and emotional well- being.

Meaningful Communication
Random acts in palliative care and end- of- life support focus on easing meaningful communication between cases, their families, and healthcare providers. These acts involve laboriously harkening to cases' stories, recollections, and enterprises, and engaging in exchanges that recognize their life gests and particular narratives. By fostering open and honest communication, healthcare providers produce openings for cases and families to partake their studies, express their wishes, and find peace during their end- of- life trip.

Supporting Families and Caregivers

Random acts in palliative care and end- of- life support extend beyond cases to their families and caregivers. These acts fete the emotional and physical risk that caregiving can have and offer support to ease their burden. Random acts may include furnishing respite care, offering emotional comforting, connecting families to support groups, or aiding with practical requirements similar as mess medication or transportation. Supporting families and caregivers promotes their well- being and enables them to give the stylish possible care for their loved bones

.

The Impact of Random Acts in Palliative Care and End- of- Life Support

Random acts in palliative care and end- of- life support have a profound impact on cases, families, and healthcare providers.

Enhanced Quality of Life Random acts contribute to the overall quality of life for cases facing serious illness or end- of- life moments. By furnishing comfort, emotional support, and moments of joy, these acts ameliorate the well- being and quality of cases, allowing them to witness peace, love, and connection during their trip.

Emotional Well- being Random acts in palliative care and end- of- life support palliate emotional torture, anxiety, and loneliness endured by cases and their families. These acts offer emotional support, confirmation, and fellowship, furnishing solace and comfort during delicate times. Emotional well- being enhances adaptability, promotes acceptance, and allows individualities to find meaning and purpose in their end- of- life trip.

relief of Caregiver Burden Random acts that support families and caregivers reduce the burden and stress associated with minding for a loved one facing serious illness or end- of- life. By furnishing support and respite, these acts enable caregivers to recharge, address their own requirements, and continue furnishing care from a place of strength and well- being.

Positive recollections and Legacy Building Random acts produce positive recollections and openings for cases and

families to make a meaningful heritage.
By engaging in exchanges, recognizing
cases' life stories, and easing meaningful
gests , these acts contribute to the
creation of lasting recollections and
support families in chancing check and
comfort after their loved bone
has passed away.

Chapter 12: Triumph over Adversity: Inspiring Stories of Medical Miracles

Introduction:

Medical cautions are admiration-inspiring events that showcase the remarkable adaptability of the mortal spirit and the inconceivable advancements in ultramodern drug. These stories illustrate triumph over adversity, as individualities face putatively invincible medical challenges and crop victorious against all odds. This essay delves into the witching world of medical cautions, exploring inspiring stories that demonstrate the power of determination, invention, and the human will to overcome adversity through medical intervention.

Understanding Medical Cautions

Medical cautions relate to extraordinary and unanticipated reclamations or issues in the face of severe medical conditions or dire vaticinations. These cases challenge conventional medical prospects and defy the boundaries of what was formerly supposed possible. Medical cautions frequently involve innovative treatments, cutting- edge technologies, and the unvarying fidelity of healthcare professionals, all working in accord to produce extraordinary issues.

Inspiring Stories of Medical Cautions

Remarkable reclamations from Life- Hanging Injuries Some medical cautions involve individualities who have endured severe accidents or injuries, defying prognostications of endless disability or indeed death. These stories showcase the power of adaptability, as cases suffer rigorous medical interventions, recuperation, and particular determination to reclaim their lives. From recovering from traumatic brain injuries to recovering mobility after spinal cord damage, these stories punctuate the triumph of the mortal spirit over adversity.

Successful Organ Transplants Organ transplants represent inconceivable medical cautions that save innumerous lives. The stories of individualities who admit life- saving organ transplants showcase the stopgap and adaptability that comes with the gift of a new parcel on life. These stories frequently involve not only the skill and moxie of surgeons but also the selflessness of organ benefactors and their families, illustrating the power of humanity and the profound impact of organ transplantation on individualities and their loved bones

.

Defying the Odds with Cancer remittals Cancer remittals against all odds are particularly inspiring medical cautions. These stories demonstrate the inconceivable progress made in cancer treatments, showcasing cases where individualities have overcome dire vaticinations and defied statistical prospects. From battling aggressive forms of cancer to achieving complete absolution after being supposed incorrigible, these stories emphasize the significance of stopgap, adaptability, and innovative treatments in the face of cancer.

Miraculous reclamations from Rare conditions Medical cautions frequently involve individualities who have been diagnosed with rare and enervating conditions. These stories punctuate the inexhaustible sweats of healthcare professionals, experimenters, and lawyers who work together to find innovative treatments and implicit cures. The remarkable reclamations and bettered quality of life endured by cases with rare conditions offer stopgap to others facing analogous conditions, demonstrating the inconceivable impact of medical advancements and fidelity.

Life- Changing Surgical Interventions Complex surgical interventions can lead to transformative medical cautions. From successful organ transplants to intricate procedures that correct natural anomalies or restore mobility, these stories illustrate the power of surgical invention and moxie in transubstantiating lives. The triumph over adversity witnessed in these cases serves as a testament to the inexhaustible sweats of surgeons, medical brigades, and the insuperable spirit of cases.

The Impact of Medical Cautions

Renewed Hope and Inspiration Medical cautions give a renewed sense of stopgap and alleviation for individualities facing grueling medical conditions. These stories demonstrate that indeed in the face of adversity, there's eventuality for unanticipated and extraordinary issues. Medical cautions serve as lights of stopgap, fueling sanguinity and determination in cases, their families, and healthcare professionals likewise.

Advancement of Medical Knowledge Medical cautions frequently push the boundaries of medical knowledge and pave the way for new treatments, curatives, and exploration. These extraordinary issues challenge the being medical understanding, encouraging experimenters and healthcare professionals to explore innovative approaches and expand the realm of possibilities for cases facing analogous conditions.

Enhanced Collaboration and Advocacy
The impact of medical cautions extends beyond individual cases to foster collaboration, mindfulness, and advocacy. These stories encourage healthcare professionals, experimenters, and associations to unite, partake knowledge, and advocate for bettered access to innovative treatments. They inspire the medical community to continue pushing boundaries and seeking for better issues for all cases.

Emotional Healing and Resilience Medical cautions give emotional mending and adaptability for cases and their families. These stories offer solace and comfort, pressing the eventuality for miraculous issues and reminding individualities that they aren't alone in their struggles. The triumph over adversity demonstrated in medical cautions instills a sense of adaptability, determination, and the belief that anything is possible.

Chapter 13: Innovations in Kindness: Technological Advances in Healthcare

Introduction:

In recent times, technological advancements have revolutionized colorful diligence, and the healthcare sector is no exception. From bettered diagnostics to substantiated treatments, technology has played a pivotal part in enhancing patient care and issues. still, beyond the medical operations, technology has also fostered an terrain of kindness within healthcare. In this composition, we will explore the innovative ways technology has contributed to promoting empathy, compassion, and overall case well- being, steering in a new period of care and support.

Telemedicine and Remote Case Monitoring
One of the most significant advancements in healthcare technology is the arrival of

telemedicine. Telemedicine allows cases to consult healthcare professionals ever, breaking the walls of distance and limited access to care. This technology has opened up doors for cases in pastoral areas, those with mobility issues, and individualities with habitual ails who bear regular check- ups. By barring the need for trip and furnishing real- time videotape consultations, telemedicine promotes kindness by icing cases admit the care they need from the comfort of their homes.

also, remote patient monitoring systems have gained traction, allowing healthcare providers to keep track of cases' vital signs and health data ever. This technology offers a nonstop connection between cases and healthcare professionals, allowing for timely interventions and visionary care. By covering cases' conditions ever, healthcare providers can help complications and reduce sanitarium readmissions, eventually perfecting patient issues and quality of life.

Virtual Reality for Pain Management

Chronic pain is a enervating condition that affects millions of individualities worldwide. still, advancements in virtual reality(VR) technology have opened up new avenues for pain operation. VR systems produce immersive gests that distract cases from their pain by transporting them to virtual surroundings. This technology has proven to be effective in colorful healthcare settings, from aiding with pain relief during medical procedures to managing habitual pain conditions.

VR technology promotes kindness by furnishing cases with anon-invasive and medicine-free volition for pain operation. It offers a sense of control and commission, allowing individualities to share laboriously in their treatment. By reducing reliance on traditional pain specifics, VR technology mitigates the threat of dependence and the associated side goods, thereby fostering case well-being and overall kindness in healthcare.

Artificial Intelligence(AI) and Machine Learning
Artificial Intelligence(AI) and Machine literacy(ML) have surfaced as important

tools in healthcare, revolutionizing diagnostics, treatment planning, and patient care. AI algorithms can dissect vast quantities of medical data to identify patterns, prognosticate issues, and help healthcare providers in making informed opinions.

In terms of kindness, AI and ML technologies have significantly impacted internal health care. Chatbots and virtual sidekicks powered by AI can give emotional support, offer managing strategies, and direct individualities to applicable coffers. These tools help reduce the smirch associated with internal health, making it easier for individualities to seek help. also, AI-powered algorithms can dissect speech and textbook to identify signs of torture or suicidal creativity, enabling timely interventions and potentially saving lives.

Wearable Technology for Personalized Care

Wearable technology, similar as fitness trackers, smartwatches, and biosensors, has gained fashionability in recent times. These bias prisoner precious data about druggies' health and conditioning, allowing individualities to cover their own well- being laboriously. In healthcare settings, wearable technology offers substantiated care and empowers cases to take charge of their health.

By collecting real- time data on vital signs, sleep patterns, and physical exertion, wearable bias enable healthcare providers to gain deeper perceptivity into cases' overall health. This information facilitates early discovery of health issues and empowers individualities to make necessary life changes. likewise, wearable technology encourages cases to engage in preventative care, fostering a culture of kindness by promoting heartiness and visionary health operation.

Chapter 14: Stories from the Frontline: Random Acts of Medicine during Crisis

Introduction:

During times of extremity, healthcare professionals are frequently at the van, working lifelessly to give care and support to those in need. Amidst the chaos and query, acts of kindness and compassion shine through, demonstrating the unvarying fidelity and selflessness of these frontline icons . In this composition, we will claw into the stories of arbitrary acts of drug that have surfaced during colorful heads, pressing the profound impact they've had on individualities and communities.

The Hurricane Relief sweats
In the fate of a ruinous hurricane, healthcare professionals rally together to give immediate medical backing and aid to affected communities. In these dire situations, arbitrary acts of drug come

pivotal lifelines for those who have lost everything. Stories pullulate of medical brigades setting up new conventions in disaster- stricken areas, offering important- demanded medical care, vaccinations, and distributing essential inventories.

One similar story comes from a croaker who donated in Puerto Rico after Hurricane Maria. She worked lifelessly to give medical care to remote and isolated communities that had been cut off from access to healthcare. Alongside her medical platoon, they treated a range of conditions, from minor injuries to habitual ails, and handed emotional support to individualities traumatized by the disaster. These acts of drug, born out of compassion and a sense of duty, helped restore stopgap and mending to those in hopeless need.

Healthcare in War Zones
In war- torn regions, healthcare systems are frequently disintegrated, leaving civilians vulnerable and in hopeless need of medical attention. In these harrowing circumstances, stalwart medical professionals risk their lives to deliver

critical care, frequently working with limited coffers and under constant trouble.

One inspiring story surfaced from a croaker
who donated in a war zone. Despite the constant peril and the failure of inventories, this croaker
and their platoon performed innumerous surgeries, treated wounded dogfaces and civilians, and handed medical aid to displaced families. Their acts of drug, carried out amidst the chaos of war, offered a hint of stopgap and comfort to those affected by the conflict, demonstrating the adaptability and fidelity of healthcare professionals in the face of unconceivable challenges.

Pandemic icons
The COVID- 19 epidemic brought healthcare professionals to the van, battling an unnoticeable adversary while risking their own lives. In the midst of overwhelmed hospitals and unknown pressure, stories of arbitrary acts of drug surfaced as lights of light in dark times.

One similar story revolves around a nanny who donated to work in a COVID-19 ferocious care unit. Despite the inviting workload and the fear of contracting the contagion, this nanny went over and beyond to give care and support to cases. From holding the hands of insulated individualities to easing virtual calls with their families, these acts of drug handed comfort and solace to cases and their loved bones
amidst the insulation assessed by the epidemic.

Supporting Vulnerable Populations
During times of extremity, vulnerable populations similar as the homeless, deportees, and marginalized communities are disproportionately affected. In these cases, healthcare professionals play a pivotal part in icing indifferent access to care and championing for the most vulnerable.

An inspiring story surfaced from a croaker
who established a mobile clinic to give healthcare services to homeless individualities in their megacity. The croaker

and their platoon handed introductory medical care, distributed hygiene accoutrements , and connected individualities with social services for long- term support. These arbitrary acts of drug not only addressed immediate healthcare requirements but also demonstrated a deep understanding of the underpinning social determinants of health, promoting kindness and inclusivity in the face of extremity.

Chapter 15: From Strangers to Lifesavers: Recounting Organ Donation Acts

Introduction:

Organ donation is a remarkable act of compassion and liberality that saves lives and provides stopgap to individualities in dire need of organ transplants. Each time, innumerous nonnatives make the selfless decision to contribute their organs, offering a alternate chance at life to donors and their families. In this composition, we will claw into the inconceivable stories of organ donation acts, relating the peregrinations of individualities who went from being nonnatives to getting true lifesavers.

The Gift of Life A Mother's Love
One of the most important stories of organ donation revolves around a mama who lost her youthful child in a woeful accident. Devastated by the loss, she made the valorous decision to contribute

her child's organs, allowing other children to live and thrive.

The impact of her decision was felt profoundly when a youthful boy entered her child's heart. He'd been staying desperately for a heart transplant, and this selfless act saved his life. Through the mama 's extraordinary act of love, her child's heritage lived on, and another family was granted the gift of their child's twinkle. This story serves as a testament to the power of organ donation, turning grief into stopgap and love into life.

A Bond Beyond Blood Sisters United
The bond between siblings is frequently described as unbreakable, and this sentiment holds true in the realm of organ donation. One inspiring story tells of two sisters, one in hopeless need of a order transplant and the other stepping forward as a living patron.

The philanthropist family had been battling order failure, and his health was deteriorating fleetly. In an extraordinary display of fraternal love, the other stock offered his order without vacillation. The transplant was a success, and the philanthropist recaptured his health and quality of life. The bond between the sisters grew stronger, fueled by the participated experience of giving and entering the gift of life. This story exemplifies the inconceivable impact that organ donation can have within families, forging an unbreakable connection and offering a new parcel on life.

nonnatives United by a Common thing In numerous cases, organ donation acts bring together complete nonnatives who are bound by a common purpose- to save lives. These important stories punctuate the profound impact of altruism and compassion in the face of adversity.

One similar story recounts the trip of a youthful woman who suffered from a severe liver complaint. As her health deteriorated, she was put on the transplant staying list, hoping for a phenomenon. That phenomenon came in the form of a foreigner who, upon learning about her condition, selflessly bestowed a portion of their liver. The transplant was successful, and the youthful woman's life was ever changed. The inconceivable act of a foreigner's kindness not only saved her life but also inspired her to pay it forward, getting an advocate for organ donation and raising mindfulness about the significance of giving the gift of life.

A heritage of Hope Honoring Loved Bones Organ donation acts frequently come a way to recognize the memory and heritage of loved bones
who have passed away. These acts give solace and a sense of purpose amidst grief, as families find comfort in knowing that their loved bones
continue to make a difference in the lives of others.

One poignant story revolves around a family who tragically lost their son in a auto accident. Despite the desolation, they set up solace in giving her organs, allowing others to live on through her gift. Times latterly, they connected with the donors of their son's organs, forming deep and meaningful connections. The donors expressed their gratefulness and participated stories of how their lives had been converted by the gift they had entered. Through this act of organ donation, the family set up mending and a sense of purpose in recognizing their son's life.

Chapter 16: Spreading the Spirit of Healing: How Random Acts of Medicine Inspire Change

Introduction:

Random acts of drug are important demonstrations of compassion, kindness, and selflessness within the healthcare field. These acts go beyond the regular practice of drug, offering support, comfort, and mending to individualities and communities in unanticipated ways. From small gestures of kindness to large-scale enterprise, arbitrary acts of drug have the eventuality to inspire change, fostering a culture of empathy, adaptability, and stopgap. In this composition, we will explore how these acts of drug spread the spirit of mending and bring about positive metamorphoses.

Cultivating Compassion

Random acts of drug serve as monuments that healthcare isn't just about treating medical conditions; it's about minding for the whole person. These acts cultivate compassion and empathy among healthcare professionals, inspiring them to go beyond their clinical duties and truly connect with their cases.

One illustration of a arbitrary act of drug is when a nanny , feting the emotional torture of a case, takes the time to sit with them, hear to their enterprises, and offer words of comfort. This simple act of mortal connection can have a profound impact, easing anxiety, reducing passions of insulation, and breeding a sense of trust between the case and the healthcare provider.

When healthcare professionals constantly engage in acts of kindness and compassion, it creates a ripple effect, inspiring others to follow suit. By fostering a culture of empathy and understanding, these acts lay the foundation for meaningful change in healthcare settings, where the emotional well- being of cases becomes as important as their physical health.

Empowering Cases
Random acts of drug have the power to empower cases, making them active actors in their own healthcare trip. By fostering a sense of trust and collaboration, healthcare professionals can inspire cases to take charge of their health and make informed opinions.

For case, a croaker
who takes the time to explain treatment options, hear to cases' enterprises, and involve them in decision- timber can significantly impact patient issues. This act of drug encourages cases to endorse for themselves, ask questions, and laboriously share in their care. By empowering cases, healthcare providers produce a sense of power and responsibility, eventually leading to better health issues and increased patient satisfaction.

likewise, acts of drug that give cases with educational coffers, support groups, or access to community programs can also empower individualities to take control of their health. These enterprise enable cases to seek knowledge, find support, and make positive changes in their cultures. By empowering cases, arbitrary acts of drug contribute to long- term well-being and inspire individualities to come lawyers for their health and the health of others.

Breaking walls and Addressing difference Random acts of drug can also be catalysts for change in addressing healthcare difference and breaking down walls to pierce. In numerous communities, individualities face obstacles similar as fiscal constraints, lack of transportation, or language walls that help them from entering acceptable healthcare.

Acts of drug that target these walls can have a profound impact on marginalized communities. For illustration, a group of healthcare professionals organizing free health conventions in underserved areas can give important- demanded care to those who would else go without. By bringing healthcare directly to these communities, these acts of drug ground the gap in access, making healthcare services more indifferent.

also, acts of drug that address language walls, artistic perceptivity, and social determinants of health can contribute to reducing difference. For case, healthcare professionals who give culturally competent care, offer restatement services, or unite with community associations can insure that healthcare is accessible and inclusive for all.

Inspiring Future Generations
Random acts of drug have the power to inspire the coming generation of healthcare professionals. By witnessing acts of kindness and compassion, aspiring croakers
, nursers, and other healthcare providers are motivated to follow in the steps of those who came before them.

Through mentorship programs, shadowing gests , and exposure to arbitrary acts of drug, youthful individualities gain immediate knowledge of the impact they can have on the lives of others. These gests inspire them to pursue careers in healthcare and inseminate in them a deep commitment to empathy, compassion, and case-centered care.

likewise, acts of drug that involve community engagement and outreach programs give openings for scholars to laboriously share in addressing healthcare requirements. By engaging in these enterprise, youthful individualities learn the significance of service, social responsibility, and advocacy, laying the root for a generation of healthcare professionals who prioritize the well-being of their cases and communities.